A COLLECTION
OF MEDIEVAL SONGS

Design: Nate Berry

TABLE OF CONTENTS

Special thanks to Nate and Xander and to my family and friends whose support made this book possible.

INTRODUCTION

Dear Musician,

This collection of Medieval and Early Renaissance sheet music is only a tiny sampling of the wide variety of musical styles enjoyed in Western Europe between 1100 and 1600 AD. Thousands of songs have survived in written manuscripts and in the form of traditional folk tunes. There were love ballads, epic war carols, fast-paced dances, religious chants and more!

None of these songs were intended to be played on the piano because it didn't exist! Most of them contained only one or two written melodies or didn't have any musical accompaniment at all. Some creative license has been taken to adapt them to be played and enjoyed as solos. I have worked hard to preserve all of the original notes and capture the intended spirit of the songs, while also writing notation for late intermediate-level pianists.

I encourage you to read the information page attached to each song. You will learn a little bit about ancient composers and music theory as well as find occasional tips to help you interpret the mood of each piece. Notated dynamics and phrasing are minimal to allow for personal expression. You will also find images of authentic medieval artwork and original lyrics along with their English translations.

I sincerely hope that you will love these songs as much as I do and gain a new appreciation for medieval music!

Sincerely,

Sarah Berry

O Ignee Spiritus

12th Century Germany   **Mode: F Dorian**

HILDEGARDIS *a Virgin Prophetes, Abbes of*
S.t Rvperts Nunnerye. She died at Bingen A° Do:
1180. Aged 82 yeares.
W. Marshall sculpsit.

Hildegard von Bingen (1098-1179) is one of the earliest known composers of Europe. Hildegard founded a nunnery and was not only a gifted composer, but also wrote books on medicine and natural history.

This Gregorian *plainchant*, a type of early Christian hymn, is dedicated to the Holy Spirit. The arrangement includes only the first four of the thirteen Latin verses. As most chants of the era were, "O Ignee Spiritus" is *monophonic* (one melody) and would have likely been sung *a cappella* by women or men in unison. At most, a small portable organ might have played a single note as a sort of drone, but chants were almost always unaccompanied vocals.

This chant is very heavy on *melisma*, meaning one word or syllable is held out and sung over many tones. The acoustics in the vaulted cathedral ceilings would have made a very haunting and otherworldly impression on the audience.

O ignee Spiritus, laus tibi sit,
qui in timpanis et citharis
operaris.

Mentes hominum de te flagrant
et tabernacula animarum eorum
vires ipsarum continent.

Inde voluntas ascendit
et gustum anime tribuit,
et eius lucerna est desiderium.

Intellectus te in dulcissimo sono
advocat ac edificia tibi
cum racionalitate parat, que in aureis
operibus sudat.

English Translation

O fiery Spirit, praise to you,
who on the tympana and lyre
work and play!

By you the human mind is set ablaze,
the tabernacle of its soul
contains its strength.

So mounts the will
and grants the soul to taste—
desire is its lamp.

In sweetest sound the intellect
upon you calls,
a dwelling-place prepares for you,
with reason sweating in the golden labor.

O Ignee Spiritus

Hildegard von Bingen, (1098-1179)
Arr. Sarah Berry

Freely, with feeling. Do not rush.　(=60)

la a ni ma rum e o rum vi res ip sa rum - - - - - con - - - ti - - nent.

Un - - de vo lun - - tas a scen - - - dit et gu stum a ni mae - - - tri bu it,

et e - - lus lu - - - cer - - - - na - est - - de si - - - - - de ri - - um.

In tel - - - lec tus - - - te in - - - dul cis si mo so - - - no ad - - vo

cat - - - ac e di fi ci a - - ti bi cum - ra ci o - - na li ta te-

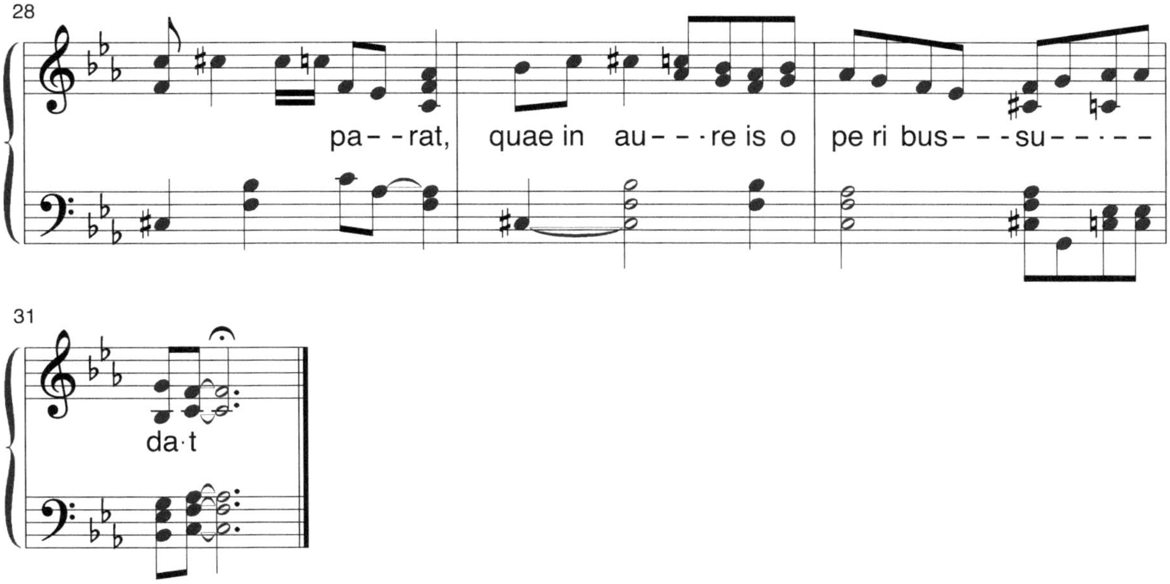
28
pa- - rat, quae in au- - - re is o pe ri bus- - - su- - - - -
31
da t

PAGE INTENTIONALLY LEFT BLANK

Como Poden Per Sas Culpas

13th Century Spain   **Mode: D Dorian**

"Como Poden" is also known as "Cantiga 166" from the *Cantigas of Santa Maria*. There are roughly 400 cantigas in this Spanish collection of beautifully illustrated religious solos. The collection is attributed to Alfonso X (el Sabio), King of Castile and Leon from 1252 to 1284, but it is unlikely he composed all of them himself.

The cantigas are all monophonic (single melody) with poetic lyrics praising the Virgin Mary. "Como Poden per sas Culpas" is written in Galician Portuguese and tells the story of Holy Mary healing a lame man in Salas.

This arrangement uses *hemiola*, which is a rhythmic switch between 6/8 and 3/4 time. Hemiola rhythms are commonly found in fast-paced Spanish and Latin music.

Como Poden per sas Culpas

Cantiga 166

Alfonso X (1221-1284)
Arr. Sarah Berry

Chorus:

Como poden per sas culpas
Os omes ser contreitos
Assi poden pela Virgen
Depois seer saos feitos

Verse I

Ond' aveo a un home
Por pecados que fezera
Que foi tolleito dos nembros
Dua door que houvéra
E durou assi cinc' anos
Que mover-se non podéra
Assi avia os nenbros
Todos do corpo maltreitos
Chorus

Verse II

Con esta enfermidade
Atan grande que avia
Prometeu que, se guarisse
A Salas logo irya
E ha livra de cera
Cad' ano ll' ofereria
E atan taste foi sao
Que non ouv' y outros preitos

Chorus:

How can it be one's fault | men
become crippled,
And thanks to the Virgin Mary,
they can be healed.

Verse I

Where there was a man, | that
for sins he had committed,
Became paralyzed and pained
and stayed like this for five years
| unable to even move,
so did his extremities | his body
injured.

Verse II

With this infirmity | so great this
man promised that, if it ceased, |
he would offer a book to a Saint
every year.
And so it was that as soon as he
became healthy, there were no
more tributes

Translation by Clarisse Offen

Palästinalied

13th Century Germany

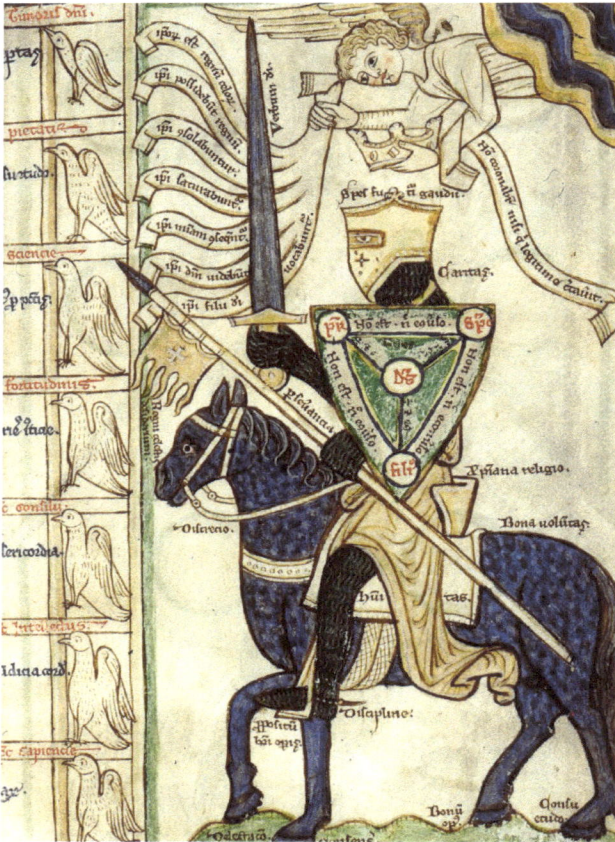

Walther von der Vogelweide (c. 1170-1230) was a very famous German poet and traveling singer (Minnesänger). This song, called "Crusader's Song" or "Song of Palestine," is the only one of his many surviving poems with a complete melody. It was written around the time of the Fifth Crusade and is sung from the point of view of a crusader seeing Christ's homeland.

There are quite a few modern versions of this song. Some are slow and steady like a march and others are very expressive. This arrangement is best played Largo or Lento (55-60 bpm).

The oldest manuscript source contains seven stanzas, but only the first two are used here. If lyrics are performed, they should begin at measure 10 and end at measure 66. Two lines from the second verse have been adapted as an optional ending.

Original German Text

Nû alrêst lebe ich mir werde,
sît mîn sündic ouge siht
daz here lant und ouch die erde,
der man sô vil êren giht.
ez ist geschehen, des ich ie bat,
ich bin komen an die stat,
dâ got menischlîchen trat.

Schoeniu lant, rîch unde hêre,
swaz ich der noch hân gesehen,
sô bist dûz ir aller êre.
waz ist wunders hie geschehen!
daz ein magt ein kint gebar,
hêre über aller engel schar,
was daz niht ein wunder gar?

sô bist dûz ir aller êre.
waz ist wunders hie geschehen!
waz ist wunders hie geschehen!

**Rhyming English Translation
(Frank Nicholson, 1907)**

Life's true worth at last beginneth,
Now my sinful eyes behold
Holy land, the earth that winneth
Fame for glories manifold.
I have won my lifelong prayer:
I am in the country where
God in human shape did fare.

Lands, the greatest, goodliest, fairest,
Many such mine eyes have seen;
O'er them all the crown thou bearest.
Think what wonders here have been!
From a Maid a babe did spring,
O'er the angel hosts a king;
Was not that a wondrous thing?

O'er them all the crown thou bearest.
Think what wonders here have been!
Think what wonders here have been!

Palästinalied

13th Century German Crusade Song

Walther von der Vogelweide
Arr. Sarah Berry

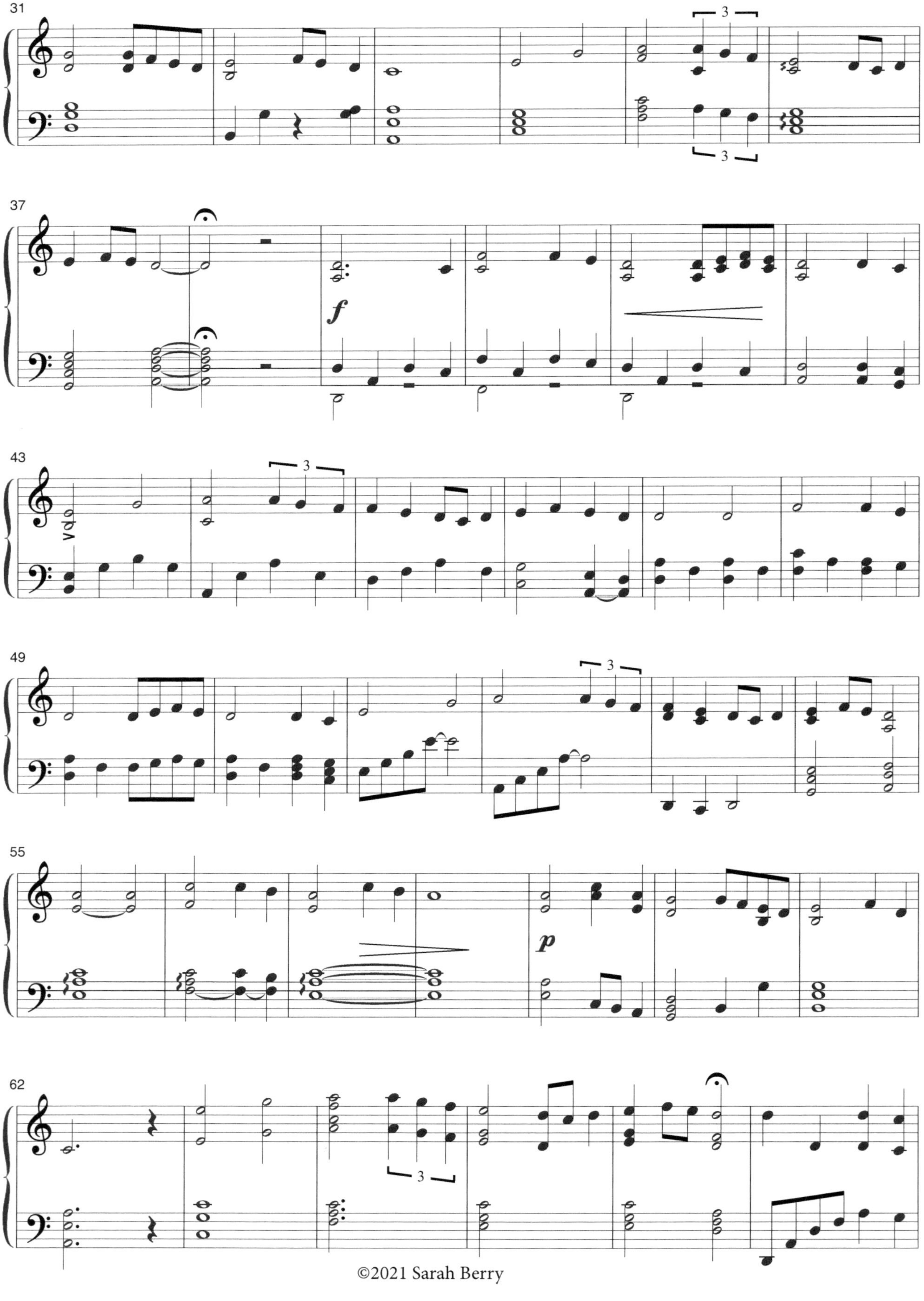
31
37
f
43
49
55
p
62

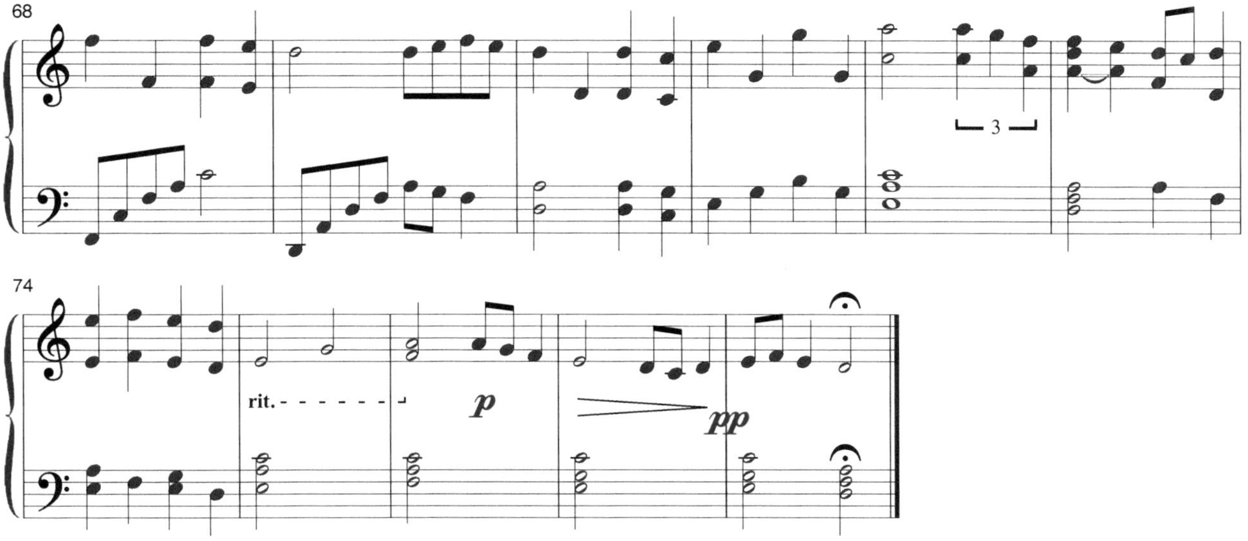
68
3
74
rit.
p
pp

PAGE INTENTIONALLY LEFT BLANK

Douce Dame Jolie

14th Century France   **Mode: D Dorian**

Guillaume de Machaut (c. 1340-1400) was the leading 14th-Century French composer of a musical style called *ars nova* that used complex rhythms and structures. This song is a monophonic *virelai*, a popular format for poetry and love songs.

Many of Machaut's songs were about courtly love and were sometimes sung by dancers. "Douce Dame Jolie" is about the unrequited love for a "sweet beautiful lady."

Douce Dame Jolie

Douce dame jolie,
Pour dieu ne pensés mie
Que nulle ait signorie
Seur moy fors vous seulement.

Qu'adès sans tricherie
Chierie
Vous ay et humblement
Tous les jours de ma vie
Servie
Sans villain pensement.

Helas! et je mendie
D'esperance et d'aïe;
Dont ma joie est fenie,
Se pité ne vous en prent.

Mais vo douce maistrie
Maistrie
Mon cuer si durement
Qu'elle le contralie
Et lie
En amour tellement

Qu'il n'a de riens envie
Fors d'estre en vo baillie;
Et se ne li ottrie
Vos cuers nul aligement.

Et quant ma maladie
Garie
Ne sera nullement
Sans vous, douce anemie,
Qui lie
Estes de mon tourment,

A jointes mains deprie
Vo cuer, puis qu'il m'oublie,
Que temprement m'ocie,
Car trop langui longuement.

English Translation

Sweet, beautiful lady
For God's sake, do not think
That anyone rules over me
But you alone

For endlessly, and without false-hood
I have cherished you
And humbly
All the days of my life
I have served you
With no unworthy thought

Alas! and I beg

For hope and aid
For my joy is ended
If you do not take pity

But your sweet mastery
Masters
My heart so harshly
That it torments
And binds it
So much in love

That it desires nothing
But to be in your service
And yet your heart
Grants it no relief

And since my sickness
Will never be healed
Without you, sweet enemy
Who is glad
At my torment

I join my hands and pray
To your heart, since it forgets me
That it should kill me quickly
For I languish too long

Douce Dame Jolie

Guillaume de Machaut (c. 1300-1377)
Arr. Sarah Berry

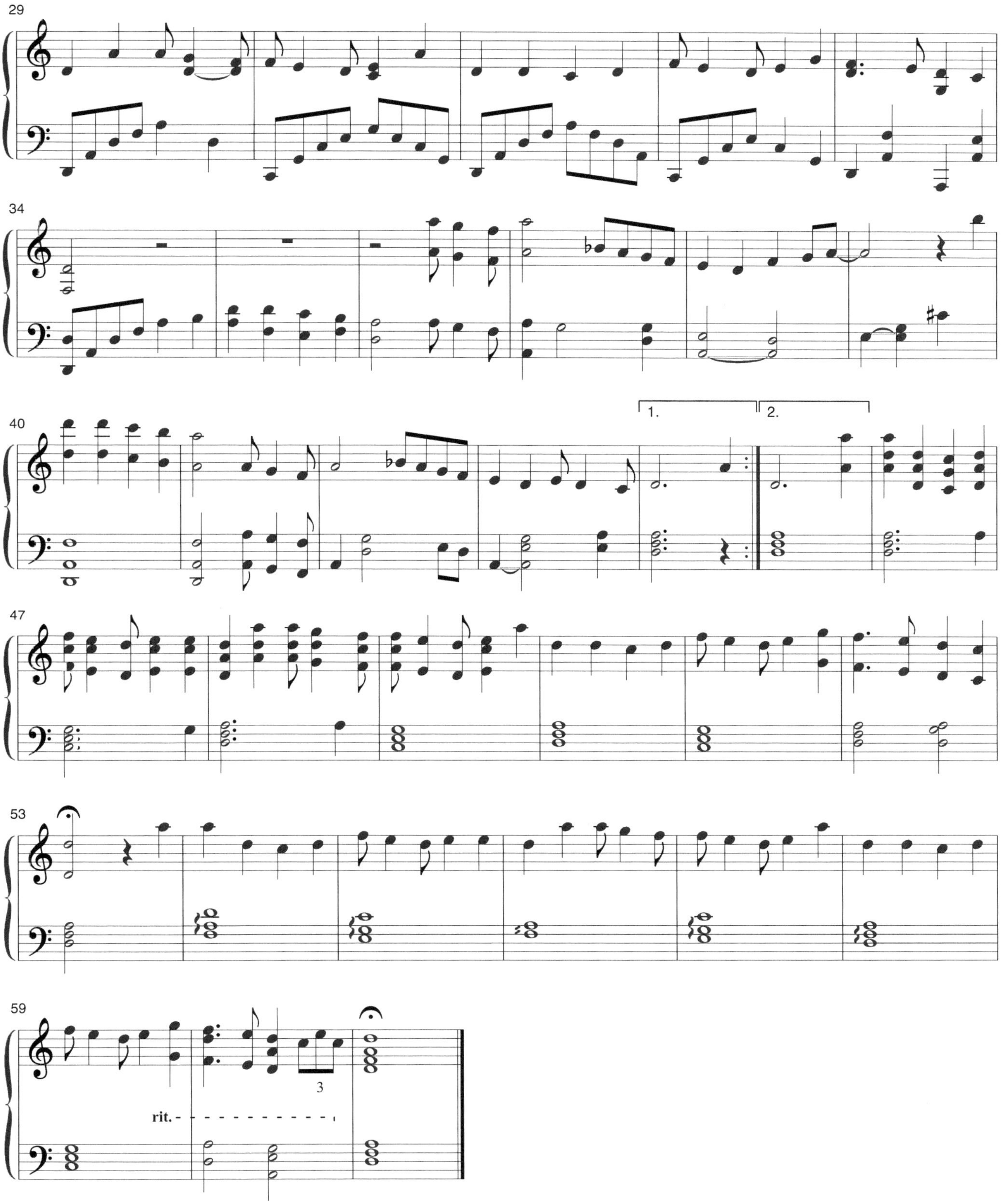
29
34
40
1.
2.
47
53
59
rit.
3

PAGE INTENTIONALLY LEFT BLANK

Ecco la Primavera

14th Century Italy   **Mode: A Aeolian**

Francesco Landini (c. 1325-1397), was one of the most influential composers of the Middle Ages. Despite being blind, he played a number of instruments, built organs and composed over 150 musical works, mostly *ballatas* and *madrigals*. The *ballata* was an artsy form of ars nova era dance music that was very popular in Italy.

"Ecco la Primavera [Spring has Come]," a two-part ballata, is a joyful celebration of Spring. This piano arrangement is a faithful adaptation of the original, with only necessary harmony added. It should be played at a very fast and lively tempo (vivace).

Ecco la Primavera

Ecco la primavera,
Che'l cor fa rallegrare,
Tempè d'annamorare
E star con lieta cera.

Noi vegiam l'aria e'l tempo
Che pur chiam' allegrezza
In questo vago tempo
Ogni cosa vaghezza.

L'erbe con gran freschezza
E fior' coprono i prati,
E gli albori adornati
Sono in simil manera.

Ecco la primavera
Che'l cor fa rallegrare
Tempè d'annamorare
E star con lieta cera.

English Translation

Spring has come
To waken hearts to gladness;
Time for lovers' madness
And to wear a happy face.

The elements together
Are beckoning to mirth;
In this delightful weather,
Delight pervades the earth.

The grass in fresh rebirth
Helps meadows come a-flower,
And every branch and bower,
Is decked with kindred grace.

Spring has come apace
To waken hearts to gladness;
Time for lovers' madness
And to wear a happy face.

Ecco la Primavera

Francesco Landini, 1396
Arr. Sarah Berry

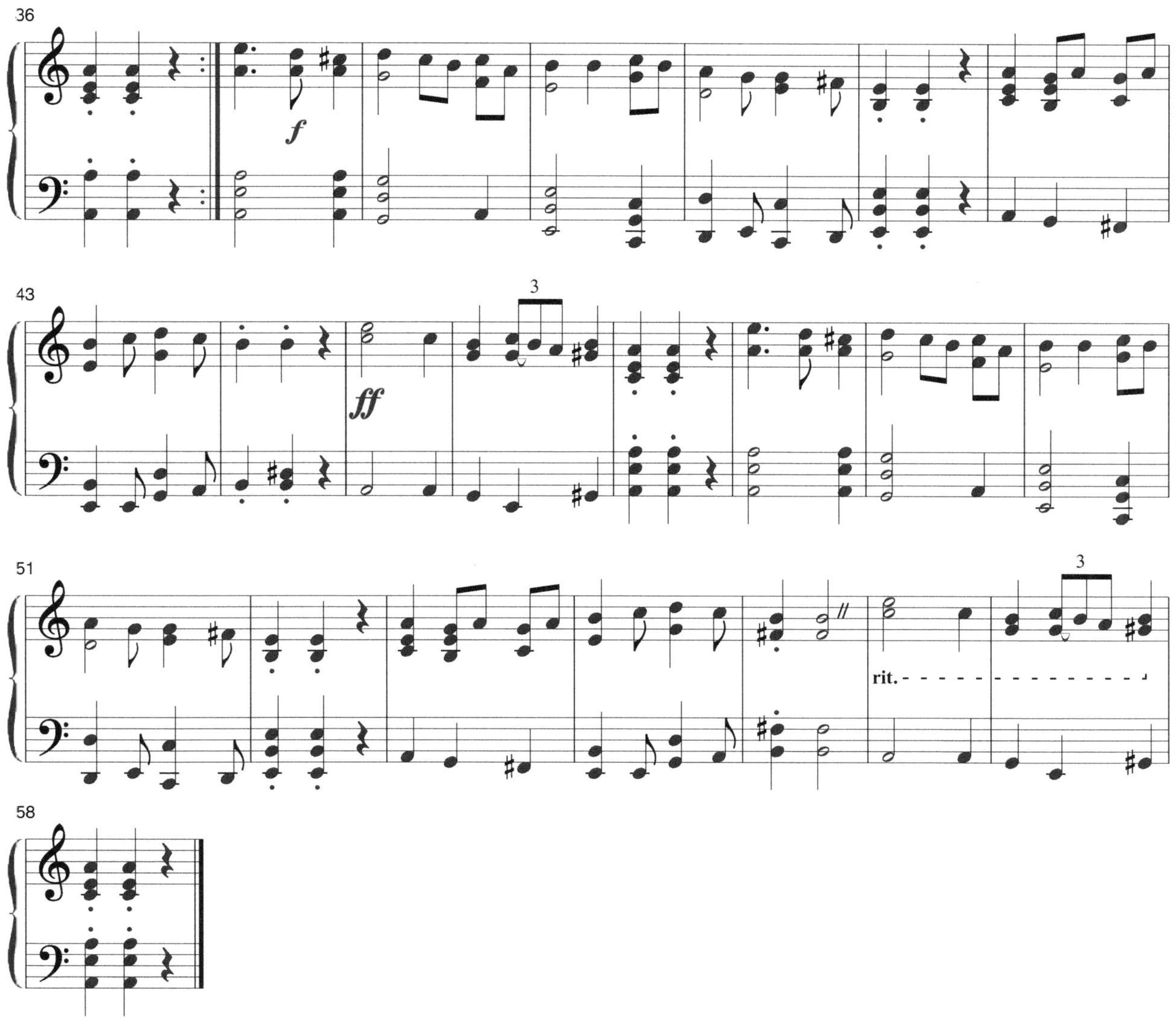
36
f
43
ff
3
51
3
rit.
58

PAGE INTENTIONALLY LEFT BLANK

Agincourt Carol

15th Century England   **Mode: G Aeolian**

Though it is technically considered a carol, this song is not related to any holiday. The "Agincourt Carol" was written to celebrate the English victory of the 1415 Battle of Agincourt. It is a celebratory hymn giving thanks to God for victory [Deo gratias Anglia redde pro victoria!]. The lyrics are written in Middle English with a short *burden* (a repeated refrain) in Latin.

The song consists of two distinct melody lines (voices) with an occasional third that joins in on the chorus. It would have most likely been performed *a capella* or with minimal instrumental accompaniment.

"Agincourt Carol" contains six verses but this version is written for only four. Each of the original melody lines have been transcribed and preserved in this unique piano arrangement.

Deo gratias anglia, redde pro victoria.

Owre kynge went forth to Normandy,
With grace and myght of chyvalry;
Ther God for hym wrought mervlusly,
Wherfore Englonde may calle and cry,
Deo gratias,
Deo gratias anglia, redde pro victoria.

He sette a sege, for sothe to say,
To Harflu toune with ryal aray;
That toune he wan and made a fray,
That Fraunce shall rewe tyl domesday.
Deo gratias,
Deo gratias anglia, redde pro victoria.

Then went owre kynge, with alle his oste,
Thorowe Fraunce for all the Frenshe boste;
He spared for drede of leste, ne most,

Tyl he come to Agincourt coste;
Deo gratias,
Deo gratias anglia, redde pro victoria.

Than for sothe that knyght comely,
In Agincourt feld he faught manly;
Thorow grace of God most myghty
He had bothe the felde, and the victory;
Deo gratias,
Deo gratias anglia, redde pro victoria.

Agincourt Carol

Anonymous, 15th century
Arr. Sarah Berry

Steady, not rushed (= 95)

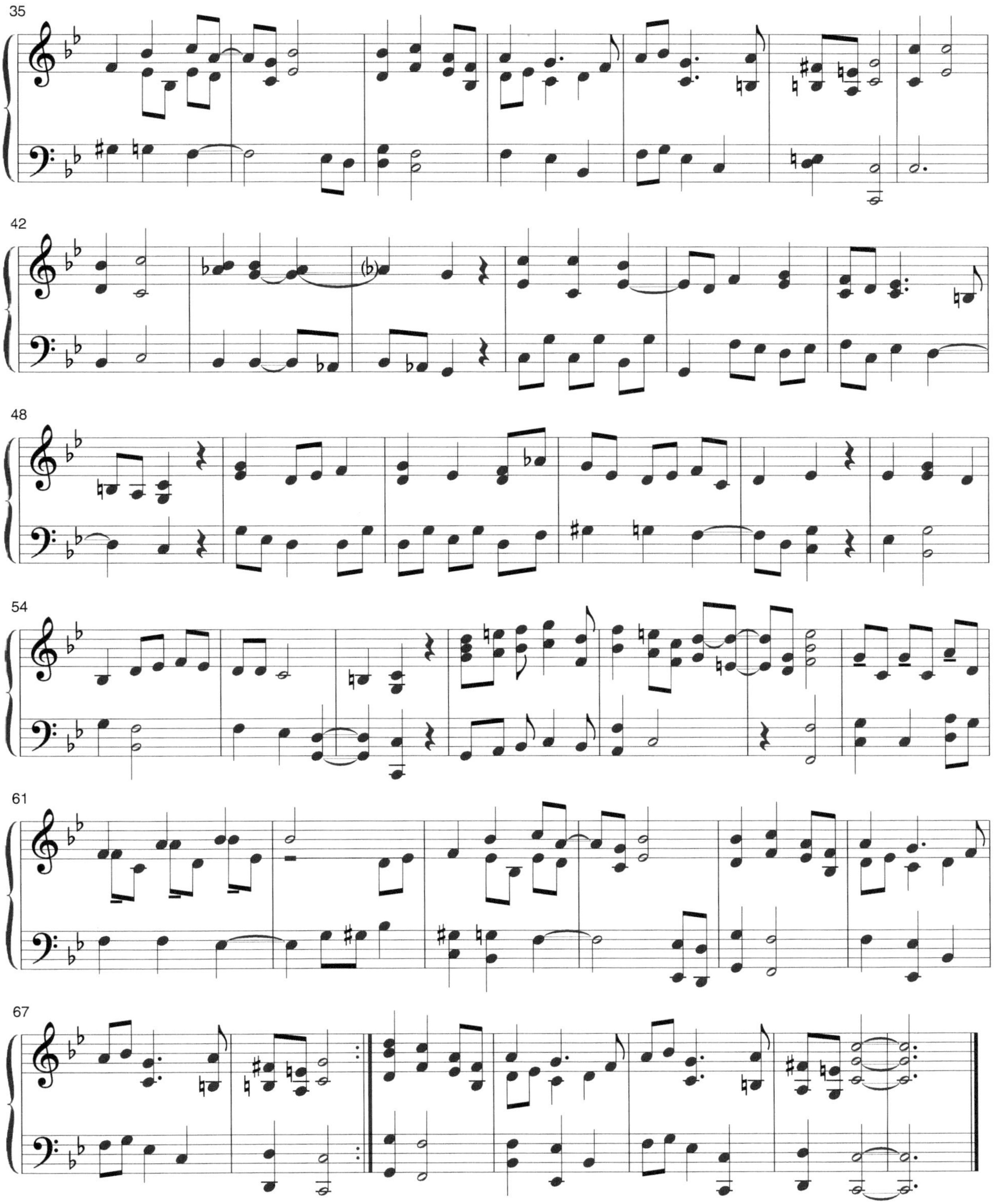
35
42
48
54
61
67

PAGE INTENTIONALLY LEFT BLANK

Ah Robyn, Gentyl Robyn

15th-16th century England   **Mode: G Aeolian**

William Cornysh (c. 1465-1523) was an actor/musician who wrote and performed in plays and composed music for the Tudor English court. He is perhaps best known for his *polyphonic* (multiple voice) love songs.

"Ah Robyn" is a madrigal that was originally performed in three-part *a cappella* with two verses being sung by a soloist over the repeated chorus. All three parts have been preserved in this instrumental adaptation.

Chorus x 3
Ah, Robin, gentle Robin,
Tell me how thy leman doth
and thou shalt know of mine.

Verse
My lady is unkind I wis,
Alack why is she so?
She lov'th another better than me,
and yet she will say no.

Chorus
Ah, Robin, gentle Robin,
Tell me how thy leman doth
and thou shalt know of mine.

Verse
I cannot think such doubleness
for I find women true,
In faith my lady lov'th me well
she will change for no new.

Chorus
Ah, Robin, gentle, Robin,
Tell me how thy leman doth
and thou shalt know of mine.

Ah Robyn, Gentyl Robyn

William Cornysh (1465-1523)
Arr. Sarah Berry

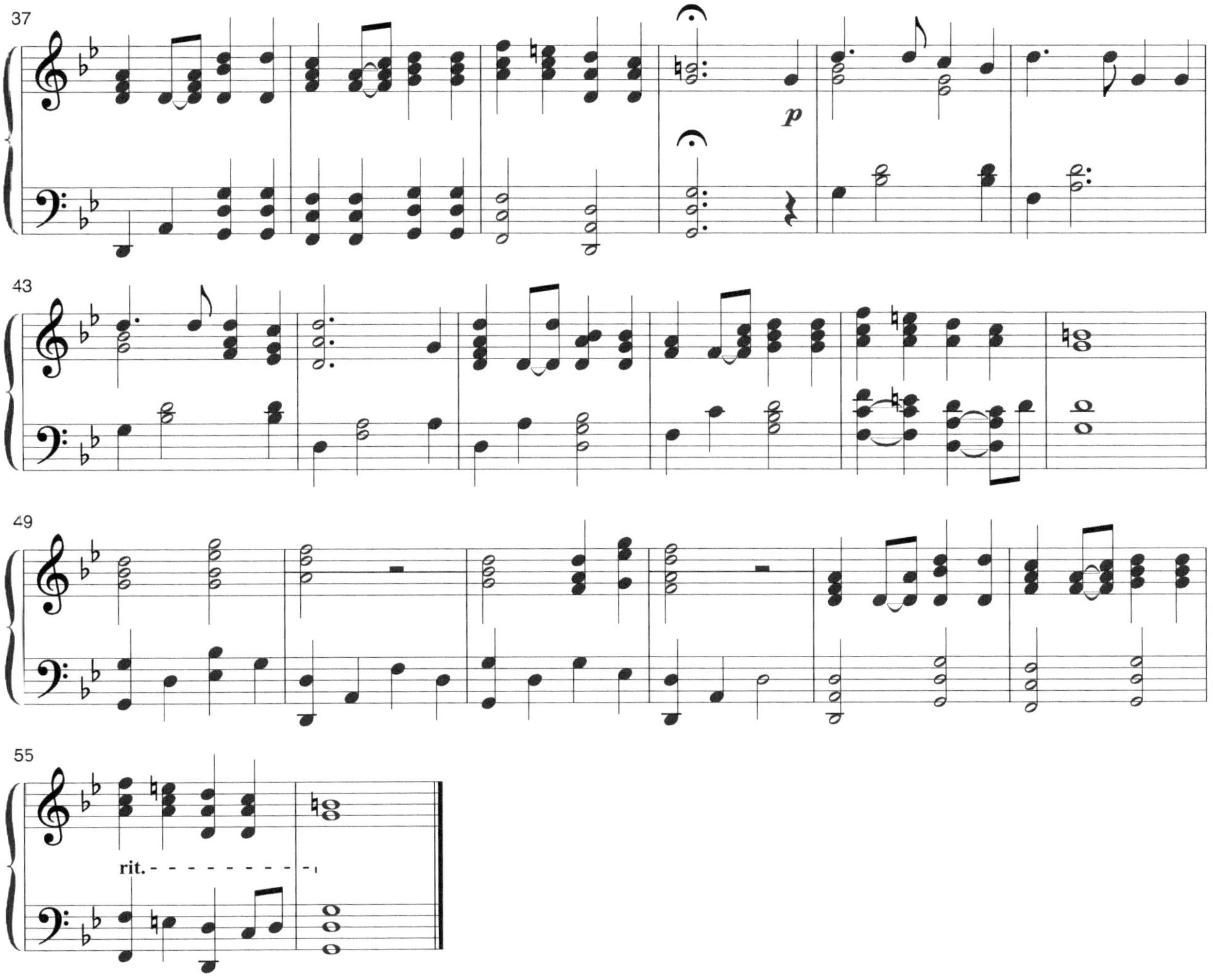
37
p
43
49
55
rit.

PAGE INTENTIONALLY LEFT BLANK

Wilson's Wilde

16th Century England   **Mode: Ionian**

The composer of this early Renaissance lute melody is unknown, but copies of it can be found in multiple locations including the *John Dowland Lute Book* (ca 1594-1600). William Byrd (1543-1623) also later published his own arrangement called "Wolsey's Wilde."

This solo is a faithful transcription of the original John Dowland melody but has been arranged to make it enjoyable to play for a late intermediate or early advanced pianist. Musical ornaments (mordents, arpeggiation) have been added to mimic the sound of a plucked string instrument.

Wilson's Wilde

Simplified arrangement in the Key of G

Anonymous, 16th Century
Arr. Sarah Berry

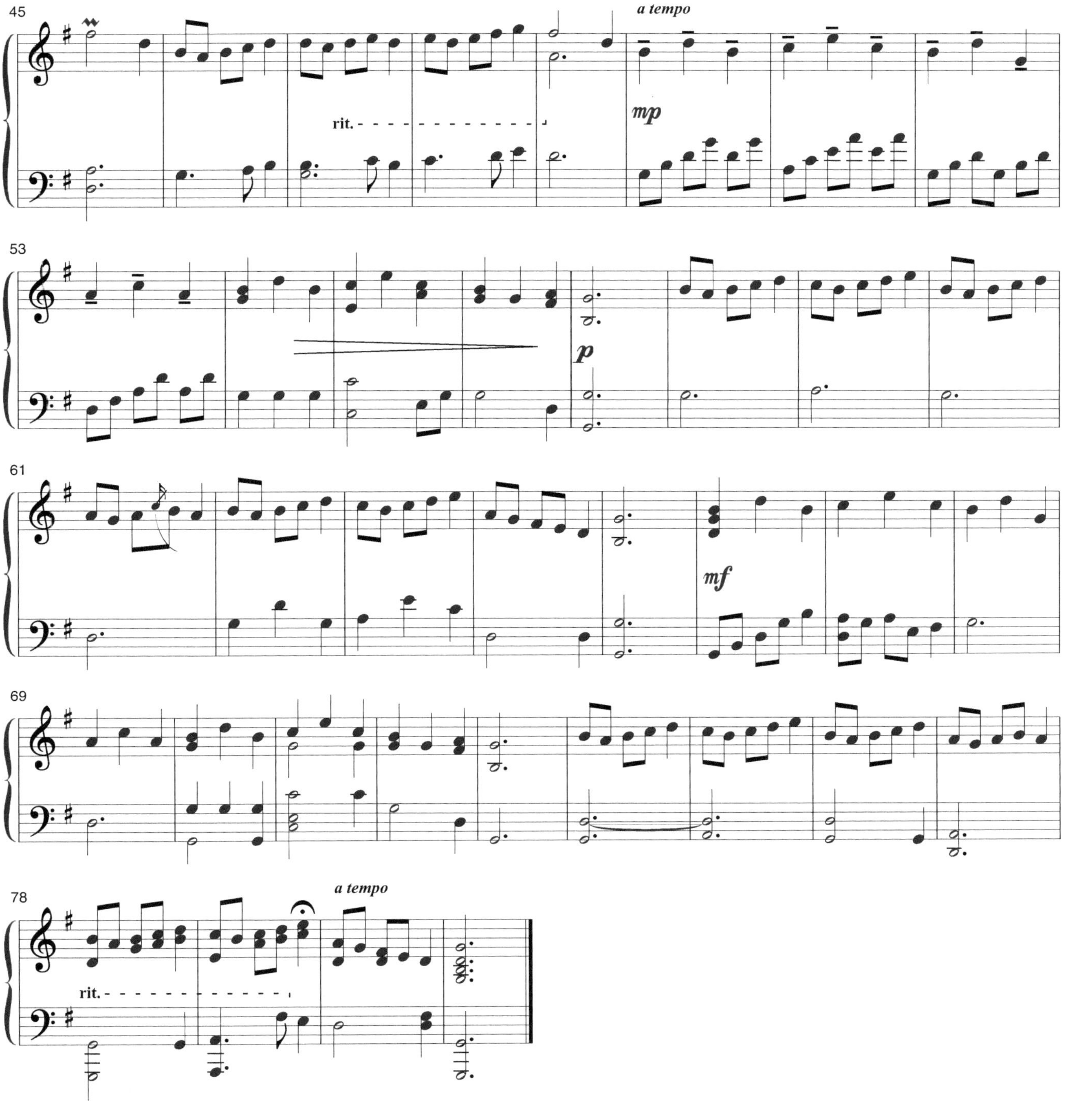
45
a tempo
rit.
mp
53
p
61
mf
69
78
a tempo
rit.

Wilson's Wilde

Original arrangement in the Key of A-flat

Anonymous, 16th Century
Arr. Sarah Berry

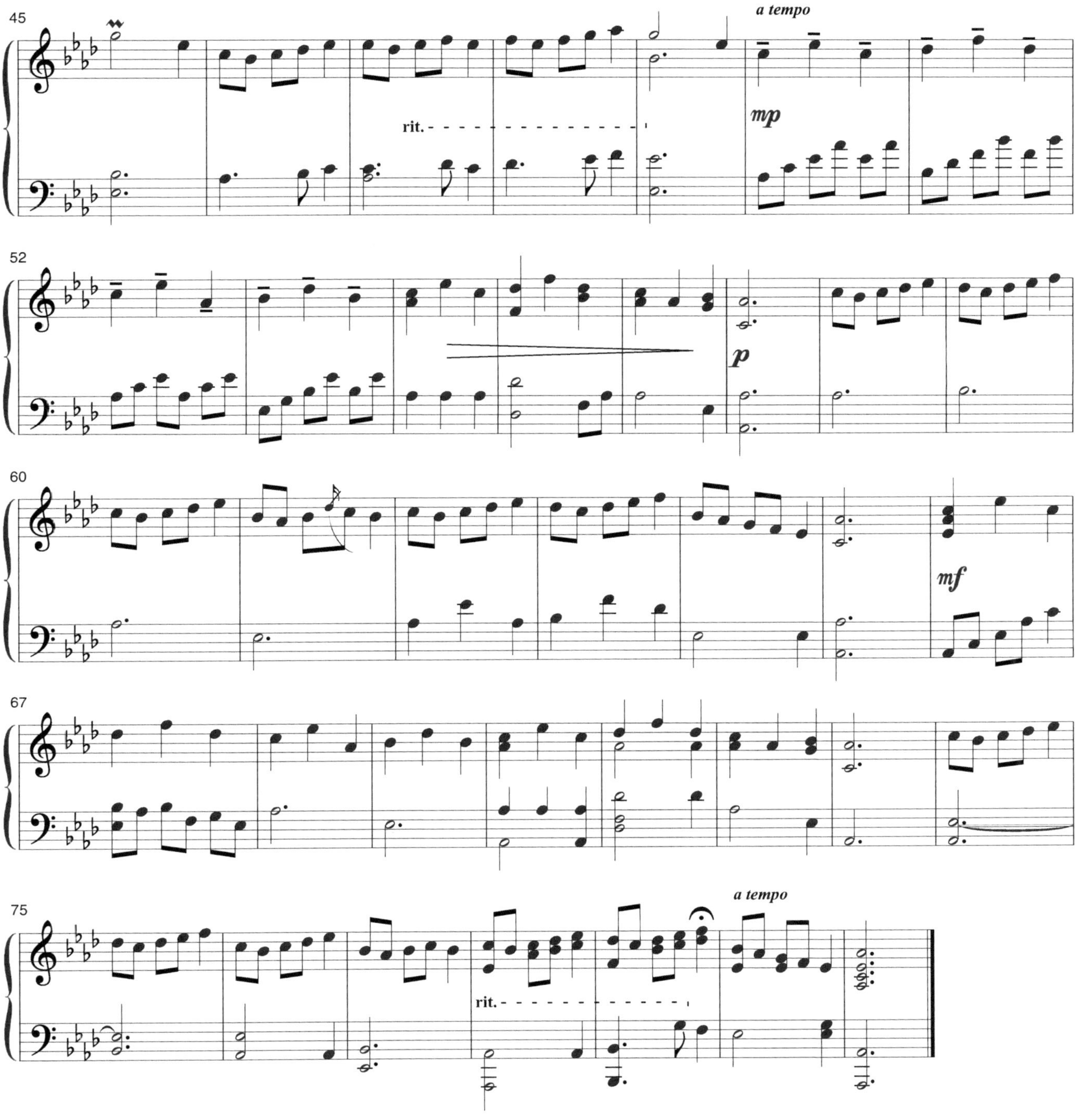
45
rit.
a tempo
mp
52
p
60
mf
67
75
rit.
a tempo

BIBLIOGRAPHY

Everist, Mark. The Cambridge Companion to Medieval Music. UK: Cambridge University Press (2011).

Loewen, Peter V. "Cantigas of Santa Maria." *Oxford Bibliographies* (Last Modified July 27, 2016). DOI: 10.1093/OBO/9780195396584-0210

Nicholson, Frank Carr. "Walther Von Der Vogelweide," in *Old German Love Songs: Translated from the Minnesingers of the 12th to 14th Centuries*. Chicago: University of Chicago Press, 1907. 71–73 https://archive.org/stream/oldgermanloveso01nichgoog#page/n142/mode/2up

Randel, Don Michael. *The Harvard Concise Dictionary of Music and Musicians* ed. Don Michael Randel. Cambridge, Mass: Harvard University Press, 1996.

Wade-Matthews, Max and Wendy Thompson. *The Encyclopedia of Music*. New York: Metro Books, 2004.

ARTWORK

All manuscript illustrations are in the public domain

Cover art :   Alfonso X, King of Castile and Leon. "Cantiga 170," *Cantigas de Santa Maria*, 1221-1284.

p. 1   Alfonso X. "Christian and Muslim Playing Ouds," *Cantigas de Santa Maria*, 1221-1284.

Music notation using Neumes. "Leaf from a Dominican Antiphoner: Resurrection" c. 1300-1325, British Library, Yates Thompson 25 MS LXXXIIIA f.1

p. 2   Marshall, William (active 1617-1650). "Hildegard of Bingen Line Engraving" London, Wellcome Library. Wellcome Images. V0002761. https://wellcomeimages.org.

p. 7   Alfonso X, "Cantiga 50," *Cantigas de Santa Maria*, 1221-1284.

p. 10   Peraldus, Guilelmus. "Peraldus Knight," *Summa de virtutibus et vitiis*, c. 1236. British Library, Harleian MS 3244 f. 28.

p. 15   Machaut, Guillaume de. "Guillaume de Machaut et Bon Espoir de Le Remède de Fortune," *Oeuvres narratives et lyriques*, 1380-1395. Paris, Bibliothèque Nationale de France, f. 27r

p. 20   "Francesco Landini," *Codex Squarcialupi*, 1410-1415. Firenze, Biblioteca Laurenziana, MS Med. Pal. 87.

Insect and Flowers. *.Book of Hours,* 1510-1525. Artwork by Jean Bourdichon. British Library, MS Additional18855 f. 21.

p. 24   "Agincourt Carol," *Trinity Carol Roll*, c.1415. Cambridge, Library of Trinity College, Trinity MS O.3.58.

p. 28   Illustration of a Robin.*The Sherborne Missal,* 1399-1407. British Library, Add MS 74236 Missal: 383.

p. 32   "Willson's Wilde," *Dowland Lute Book*, c. 1590. Folger Shakespeare Library, MS V.b.280 (olim 1610.1) f. 3r/1.

p. 37   Goose Choir. *Geese Book Vol. I.* 1503-1510. New York, Pierpont Morgan Library. MS 905 f. 186r

www.ingramcontent.com/pod-product-compliance
Lightning Source LLC
Chambersburg PA
CBHW060815090426
42737CB00002B/71